ANTHONY HOROWITZ

ANTHONY HOROWITZ

SHALINI SAXENA

ROSEN
PUBLISHING®

New York

Published in 2013 by The Rosen Publishing Group, Inc.
29 East 21st Street, New York, NY 10010

Library of Congress Cataloging-in-Publication Data

Saxena, Shalini, 1982–
Anthony Horowitz/Shalini Saxena.—1st ed.
    p. cm.—(All about the author)
Includes bibliographical references and index.
ISBN 978-1-4488-6940-4 (library binding)
1. Horowitz, Anthony, 1955– —Juvenile literature. 2. Authors, English—20th century—Biography—Juvenile literature. I. Title.
PR6058.O715Z86 2013
823'.914—dc23
[B]
                                            2011041699

Manufactured in the United States of America

CPSIA Compliance Information: Batch #S12YA: For further information, contact Rosen Publishing, New York, New York, at 1-800-237-9932.

On the cover: Anthony Horowitz poses in London at the launch of the sixth Alex Rider book, *Ark Angel*, in 2005.

CONTENTS

Every teenager has at one time or another day-dreamed about a life far removed from the pressures of school, the duties of home life, or the ceremonies of youth. Too often, we forget these dreams or dismiss them as unrealistic. For Anthony Horowitz, however, they foreshadowed the successful career he would eventually have as a writer.

Even though he was born to wealthy parents and sent to top schools in Britain, Anthony was unhappy as a child. Indeed, it was making up stories for his classmates and immersing himself in books that helped Anthony escape his troubles at school and cope with the often peculiar demands of his family. A natural storyteller, Anthony found influences for his narratives in anything from the familiar—popular culture and literature, for instance—to the unexpected, as when later in life he dreamt up characters based on a piece of pottery his wife gave him.

Like many other young boys, he was enthralled by the James Bond films of his childhood. It was fancying what it would feel like to be in Bond's shoes that sparked the idea for one of Anthony's most popular creations, the Alex Rider series, which follows the adventures of a teenage spy.

One may recognize elements of some other famous names in Horowitz's books as well. He has cited Charles Dickens, J.R.R. Tolkien, Stephen King,

nthony Horowitz poses for a portrait in Toronto during the 2006 Toronto ternational Film Festival, which included his film *Alex Rider: Operation tormbreaker*.

and C. S. Lewis as some of his many literary influences, and if read closely, one can see how he pays homage to them in his works. His Gatekeepers series (or the Power of Five, as it is known in Britain), for example, is an epic fantasy, a lot like the Lord of the Rings or the Chronicles of Narnia, except that it takes place right here on Earth.

But a gifted writer like Horowitz can take aspects of his favorite authors and turn them into something completely new and original, all the while staying true to what he believes makes for great writing. Whether his books are thrilling, macabre, fantastical, or humorous, they always engage the reader by presenting characters that he or she can relate to in some way—no matter how strange or unusual their circumstances may be.

Horowitz's creativity has allowed him time and again to captivate an audience, but perhaps as significant to his success is his drive and willingness to try his hand at all types of writing. In his career so far, Horowitz has published well over thirty books (for both children and adults), worked on nearly a dozen television shows (including several he created), and written the screenplays of three movies. And more of each are already on their way. He has also dabbled in theater and once even professed that he would like to try his hand at a game show someday! As he said in a television interview with ABC3, "It's critical that I keep myself challenged, always exploring new things."

Just by looking at the number of works credited to Horowitz and the awards he has received, it is obvious that he is committed to his craft and finding new ways to push his own limits. But after journeying with Alex Rider across the globe or battling the forces of evil with the Gatekeepers, it is easy to see why he has become as beloved as the writers that he himself adores.

ONE

HOROWITZ'S LIFE AND FAMILY

Y ou may be able to guess that Anthony Horowitz did not have a typical childhood if you hear that dinner in his house was announced by the striking of a gong or if you consider that his mother bought a human skull for him when he was thirteen (it still sits on his desk today). It may seem like the type of upbringing that would provide a future writer with plenty of material for the books he would write. And in many ways it did.

But although Horowitz grew up in a privileged household and decided that he wanted to be a writer at an early age (he says that he was certain of his future by the age of eight), he was often unhappy as a child. Teachers would criticize him and even his own father ridiculed the idea of him ever being published. Still, Horowitz was able to find confidence in his own abilities, which would allow him to get past the naysayers and rise above the obstacles he faced to become the sensation he is today.

EARLY LIFE AND FAMILY

On April 5, 1955, Anthony Craig Horowitz was born to Mark and Joyce Horowitz in Stanmore, Middlesex, England (Stanmore is an area in north London). It was an upper-class family with some memorable personalities. Anthony lived with his older brother, younger sister, and parents in a large estate called White Friars where they had several servants. In many respects, Anthony's life seemed to be from a past era. His father's strictness and his grandmother's nastiness are just some examples from the unusual childhood Anthony had. His family dinners were also quite the event. Horowitz has said that he and his siblings would not be allowed at the table if they did not provide stimulating conversation and has compared his life to *The Remains of the Day* (a 1989 novel by Kazuo Ishiguro, told from the point of view of an English butler in post–World War II England, which addresses social constraints).

Given Mark Horowitz's love of Anthony Trollope, William Makepeace Thackeray, and Victorian literature in general, it may not be too surprising that he

London, England, Anthony's lifelong home and inspiration for his future works, is seen here in 1960 from St. Paul's Cathedral.

carried himself and ran his household in a seemingly Victorian style. While it is true that he provided for his family, at least up until he died, and shared his extensive library of classic works with Anthony, Mark was always secretive and distant from his children. He once asked Anthony to ride across London to deliver £150,000 ($234,000) to a man he did not know, and even though Mark was often willing to share his wealth, he was not as generous with his praise, telling Anthony that he would never make it as a writer.

Anthony's grandmother on his mother's side, Esther Charatan, was also an unforgettable character—so much so, in fact, that he later wrote an entire book (*Granny*, 1994) based on her unpleasantness. He has described her as evil, saying she never brought joy to her family and, despite her wealth and comfort, never gave back to anyone. Much later, when she died, Horowitz said that he and his siblings actually danced on her grave.

Anthony's mother, Joyce, however, was much different. She was a socialite when Anthony was growing up, and as he describes her in the *Guardian*, "an extraordinary woman." He was close to her, and some of his most memorable moments with her include the times she would tell him stories at night. These were often stories recounting the plots of horror movies she had seen. From this, it is easy to see how Horowitz's love of horror developed and why he continues to include elements of horror in much of his writing today. It also helps explain why he asked his mother for a human skull when he was thirteen—and why she obliged by going to a medical store and buying it for him. Anthony's love of stories and storytelling would eventually help him cope with the difficulties he faced outside of the home. Only instead of listening to them, he would be the one creating them.

SCHOOLING AND EDUCATION

As a child, Anthony was terribly overweight (those unusual meals at home were often thousands of calories!), which made it hard for him to fit in anywhere. To make matters worse, he performed poorly in school and was mocked for it. Raised in a Jewish household, Anthony was sent to Sunday school at the age of eight to start preparing for his bar mitzvah. His weight and grades made him an easy target, and he said that many of the girls there were mean to him. In fact, Anthony was so scarred from the experience that in an article in the *Sunday Times*, he said he believes that "there is not a crueler species on the planet than nine-year-old girls." (He is now married, and he even created a female character, but for a long time, he did not really feel comfortable around girls.)

Unfortunately for Anthony, he did not fare much better in his regular school. When he was eight years old, he was sent away to an all-boys boarding school called Orley Farm School, located in Harrow, London. Anthony was miserable there. The headmaster would flog students and ridicule them in front of everyone (this was not, unfortunately, uncommon in many schools at the time). The other teachers were not much better and thought he was a waste of their time; in a 2003 article in the *Evening Standard*, he described them as "a motley bunch of sadists and lunatics." (Horowitz has since said that many of the villains he has created—and creatively killed off—were actually named after some of these

Charles Dickens was a major literary influence for Anthony and, along with other Victorian writers, was a favorite of his father's as well.

teachers.) Their treatment of students was so outrageous that Anthony believed that they actually enjoyed inflicting pain.

Anthony's only escape from his unhappy circumstances was making up stories. Much like many of his books today, these stories were fast-paced and full of adventure. He wanted the stories, unlike the rest of his life, to be mostly fun. He had even written his first play before the age of ten. Despite his young age, Anthony had already asked his father for a typewriter and would carry a notepad everywhere so that he could write down ideas as they came to him—he knew without a doubt that writing was what he was meant to do. For Anthony, storytelling was a sort of outlet for the frustrations he experienced in his life. As he said in one video interview

TINTIN

The Tintin comics that Horowitz adored as a child were created in 1929 by a Belgian cartoonist named Georges Rémi (1907–1983), who went by the pen name Hergé (if you reverse his initials, you get R.G., which in French, is pronounced Hergé). The first Tintin comic strip appeared in a weekly newspaper supplement for children called *Le Petit Vingtième*. The first book in the Adventures of Tintin series, called *Tintin in the Land of the Soviets*, was published not long after in 1930. There are now twenty-four Tintin books in all, although Hergé died before completing the last.

The comics chronicle the adventures of a young reporter named Tintin (a writer, as Horowitz points out, not a detective), who travels the world over accompanied by his white wire fox terrier, Snowy. His eclectic group of friends includes Captain Haddock, twin detectives named Thomson and Thompson, an opera singer named Bianca Castafiore, and Professor Cuthbert Calculus, among others.

Designed to be the perfect hero, Tintin becomes involved in cases that often endanger his life, but he never shies away from what is right. Many of his adventures actually involve real-world situations and events that were significant at the time the books were published. Always balancing excitement with a certain level of humor, it is no wonder that the Tintin adventures have been immensely popular in Europe and are still beloved around the world today.

produced by Guardian News and Media, Ltd., "There was no plan B in my life. I was going to be a writer or nothing."

Although Anthony was an avid storyteller, he has said that his love of books actually really developed after the age of eleven. When he was younger, he preferred Tintin books, which were shorter and loaded with pictures. But with their fun characters and exciting escapades, they inspired Anthony's own sense of adventure—he would even wander around museums and large homes, knocking on walls looking for the types of secret passages that Tintin would find. As Anthony got older, his love of literature increased, although he never lost his taste for adventure. He still cites the books of Willard Price, Enid Blyton, and Roald Dahl as some of his earliest influences.

Anthony finally left Orley Farm School and enrolled at Rugby School in 1968, where things began to look up for him. He made more friends and found teachers that actually inspired him. It was around this time that he began to develop his taste for the works of Charles Dickens, whom he now sees as his greatest literary inspiration. With fast-paced plots that included both social commentary and humor as well as intriguing characters, Dickens was the type of writer that Anthony aspired to be.

After he graduated from Rugby in 1973, Anthony took a year off before going to college so that he could see new parts of the world and have some adventures of his own. He spent nine months in northern Australia working as a sort of cowboy at a cattle station called Anthony Lagoon (you may recognize it from the end of *Granny*). In an interview with CITV, he stated, "I must be the only kid's writer who has killed a cow and turned it into all the different steaks."

Anthony eventually trekked through Singapore back to England, where he attended the University of York. He studied English literature in his time there and continued to write. In 1977, Anthony graduated with a bachelor of arts degree.

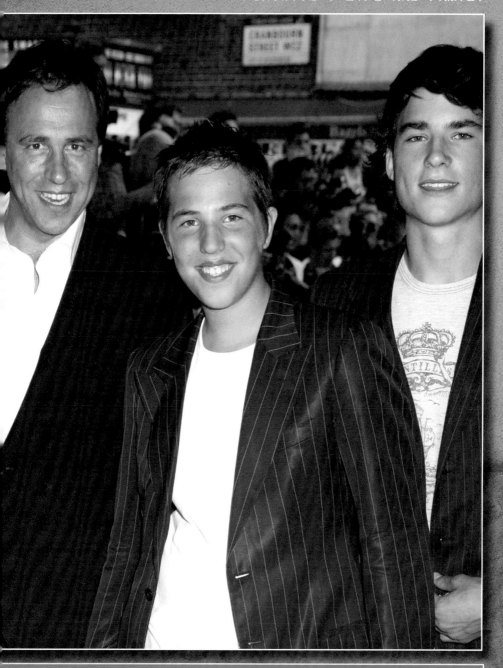

Anthony and his wife, Jill Green, pause for a photograph at the London premiere of his 2006 film, *Alex Rider: Operation Stormbreaker*.

POST-UNIVERSITY LIFE

Although Horowitz knew already that he would be pursuing a writing career after completing his studies, the path to success was not completely straightforward. Family issues and his father's mysterious dealings, for one thing, would complicate his immediate future.

Even before Mark Horowitz had Anthony riding across London on errands he did not understand, Mark had gone bankrupt and the family moved to a smaller home, this one called Tall Chys (according to the *Observer*, "chy," Horowitz said, "was supposed to be a poetic name for a chimney"). They had lost almost all their servants, but Anthony and his family still believed that Mark was wealthy. It was only after his death that they discovered that the reality was far more convoluted.

Mark, who had been battling cancer for a few years, died of a heart attack when Anthony was twenty-two years old. It turns out that Mark owed a number of banks a great deal of money. After the funeral, what ensued was Mark's wife and children desperately trying to figure out what had happened to all the wealth they thought they had. Joyce traveled to Switzerland, where Mark had apparently deposited a lot of his money, but she did not find any answers. Mark had left his only clues in a black notebook, but with strange figures and names, like Archduke and Oscar, they were impossible to decipher. The mystery—as complex as one in any of the stories Horowitz loved to read or create—was never solved.

Since Mark had even cashed in his life insurance policy before he died, Joyce owed almost everything she had and the family had to find new means of support. Joyce took up a job as a secretary, despite not having worked during her younger days. Horowitz said that she did so willingly and even cheerfully. She was later diagnosed with a terminal form of cancer, and after she died, Horowitz said that in a way, she had actually been happier in her last ten years than she had been before.

As for Horowitz, he took on a job as a copywriter (someone who writes the text in advertisements) at the prestigious advertising agency McCann Erickson, his first job after leaving York. It was here that he met his future wife, Jill Green, who was his account director. They always had a working relationship together. In fact, they would continue working together later when Horowitz began writing for television shows for which Jill served as producer.

Anthony and Jill were married in 1988 in Hong Kong. They have two sons together, Nicholas Mark (b. 1989) and Cassian James (b. 1991). They have a chocolate Labrador whose name has changed every year (he started off as Lucky, but after he survived being run over by a car, his name was changed to Unlucky, and every year after, he would have a new name). During the week, Horowitz lives in central London in an area called Clerkenwell, and he maintains a weekend home in Suffolk.

Not wanting to repeat the mistakes his parents made with him, Horowitz has maintained a very close relationship with his boys. He once told the *Evening Standard*, "All in all, my childhood was a shoebox and I was squeezed inside it: the product of what my parents wanted me to be." In contrast, he says that he would never force his kids to stay at a school they hated or do anything that made them as unhappy as he was. He acknowledges that everyone makes mistakes but hopes that his are better than the ones his parents made.

Although Horowitz clearly faced obstacles and difficulties in his past, he has also said that it is part of a writer's life to feel depressed and rejected at times, and he understands that some suffering can even be healthy for a writing career. He is also conscious of the fact that he had resources that others did not. As he said in an interview with the *Independent*, "I'm trying to avoid talking about the awful childhood I had. As people learn I came from a privileged background, their sympathy for any unhappiness I might have had is, shall we say, limited." He even once told the *Evening Standard*, "I sometimes feel I've had to overcome advantage." However you look at it, though, Anthony was surely able to overcome a great deal and conquer the insecurities that plagued him as a child. It was the process of writing that allowed him to break free from his past and become one of the most popular children's authors in the twenty-first century.

TWO

EARLY CAREER AND WORKS

While it is true that Horowitz always knew that he would be a writer, you may be surprised to learn that for many years, he did not think he would ever author any books for children. And even though his first and greatest successes have come from writing books for young adults, he does not, in fact, like the terms "children's writer" or "children's writing." What, then, happened to make Horowitz try his hand at young adult novels?

FIRST ATTEMPTS

As it turns out, Horowitz's foray into children's writing was completely unplanned. Unlike many children's book authors who started creating their works for their own children, Horowitz was unmarried and had no kids of his own. He was only twenty-two years old and happened to be bored one afternoon while at work at McCann Erickson. He jotted down ideas that came to him for the first page of a children's book and then decided to continue writing until he eventually finished the whole thing. Thus *The Sinister Secret of Frederick K. Bower* (also called *Enter Frederick K. Bower*), a story about a teenage multibillionaire, was born.

After meeting an agent at a party, Horowitz was able to get the book published in 1978. All the time he had dedicated to storytelling and writing had finally paid off, and he had proven his father wrong—there could indeed be a writer in the family after all. Horowitz wrote in the *Guardian*, "One of the saddest things for me is that [my father] died the year before my first book was accepted for publication. The notion that I become a writer was not possible to him—he ridiculed it."

Horowitz followed his first title with a few other books, also generally intended for young adults. The next publication, *Misha, the Magician and the Mysterious Amulet*, written when he was twenty-three years old, is one that he avoids discussing as he claims that it is not a very good book. Undeterred, Horowitz continued writing.

His next few attempts met with mostly modest success. Horowitz wrote four volumes of what

Even though his foray into children's literature was unplanned, Horowitz proved to have the talent to keep young readers captivated with his dazzling and inventive stories.

was to be a five-part fantasy/horror series called the Pentagram Chronicles. The series included *The Devil's Doorbell* (1983), *The Night of the Scorpion* (1984), *The Silver Citadel* (1986), and *Day of the Dragon* (1989). These, like his first two books, are now out of print. However, they have not been completely forgotten—Horowitz would later revisit the stories and themes from these volumes and turn them into some of his greatest-selling works.

RISE TO FAME

Horowitz finally found widespread recognition as a children's author after his book *The Falcon's*

Dashiell Hammett wrote the classic *The Maltese Falcon* (1930), which featured the character of Sam Spade, and influenced Horowitz's *The Falcon's Malteser* (1986).

Malteser was published in England in 1986. It follows the adventures of two brothers, Herbert and
Nick Simple, more commonly known as Tim and
Nick Diamond, respectively, who operate a detective agency. Packed with both action and humor, it
became popular in England, and Horowitz decided
to make it the first book in a series called the
Diamond Brother Mysteries. A total of seven volumes have been published so far, and both a movie
(based on the first book) and a television series
have been made. Another volume, *The Three of
Diamonds*, is a collection of three of the shorter
Diamond Brothers stories.

Part of the books' appeal is that the main characters do not take themselves too seriously. For
example, Tim Diamond, the elder of the two brothers, is rather dim and a terrible detective. He is
easily confused and is constantly making mistakes,
which can sometimes complicate the cases that he
and his much smarter younger brother, Nick, are
tackling. But it also adds a level of lightheartedness
to the sometimes dangerous situations that Tim and
Nick find themselves in.

Horowitz includes plenty of clever allusions and
a great deal of wordplay as well to keep his readers entertained throughout. Even the books' titles
contain witty references—*The Falcon's Malteser*,
for one, is a twist on the name of a classic novel

by Dashiell Hammett called *The Maltese Falcon* (1930), which was later made into a movie. Other titles in the series can also be connected to the titles of older movies and reflect Horowitz's own love of those classic stories. He even models some of the situations and dialogue in the Diamond Brothers stories after those in the films, often placing them there so that parents reading to their children can get a smile or laugh out of the books, too. The fact that these books are filled with inside jokes, codes, and messages written for his own amusement demonstrates Horowitz's sense of humor and personal investment in his writing.

The comedic elements that Horowitz included in the Diamond Brother Mysteries are also evident in some other early works of his. His book *Groosham Grange* (1988), for example, includes much of the same type of wordplay and situational humor. *Groosham Grange* and its sequel, *The Unholy Grail* (1999), which was later renamed *The Return to Groosham Grange* tell the story of David Eliot, a student at a school called Groosham Grange for young witches and wizards (keep in mind that this was well before the first Harry Potter book was published!). Although Horowitz had planned to write more books in the series, he stopped after the second.

What makes the Groosham Grange books stand out most, perhaps, is the combination of humor and horror that Horowitz adds in at almost every turn. The jokes often undercut the dramatic elements of the book, so that even when David is confronting the seemingly sinister teachers at his school, for instance, it does not feel too solemn. Moreover, Horowitz uses exaggeration to the point of absurdity sometimes to make his characters more comical. In fact, Horowitz created the characters of David's parents by greatly embellishing the qualities he saw in his own parents. Even the school itself is a reimagined version of Horowitz's own much-reviled Orley Farm School.

Granny, the book Horowitz wrote based on his own grandmother, showcases even more of his talent for exaggeration and horror. Horowitz conceived the idea for *Granny* at his grandmother's funeral and decided to try to make up for all the unhappiness she caused in her life by creating a book that would actually bring laughter and enjoyment to others. Even though he visited her regularly during the last several months before she died, he said in the *Guardian,* "It was a very weird feeling because I hated her." Published in 1994 after Horowitz had signed on with his new publisher, Walker Books, *Granny* centers around a character

GROOSHAM GRANGE VS. HOGWARTS

Horowitz has said on several occasions that J. K. Rowling's Harry Potter series, which consists of seven books about a teenage wizard named Harry Potter, made possible his own success in writing young adult novels. For a long time, it seemed that reading had fallen out of vogue with younger readers as other diversions, such as video games and the Internet, had become increasingly popular. But Rowling's books seemed to change all that as they sold over a hundred million copies worldwide and became a phenomenon among readers of all ages. This in turn led to the rise in sales of a number of other young adult novels, including those that Horowitz had authored.

It is interesting to note, however, that the first Harry Potter book, *Harry Potter and the Philosopher's Stone* (called *Harry Potter and the Sorcerer's Stone* in the United States), was actually published in England nine years after Anthony's *Groosham Grange*. On the surface, the Harry Potter books may seem to have a lot in common with the two Groosham Grange volumes, though the latter never sold as well. For example, both involve a

Fans of Harry Potter gather at a bookstore in Brookline, Massachusetts, for the midnight release of the fourth volume in the series, *Harry Potter and the Goblet of Fire*, in 2000.

special school for young wizards and witches, which cannot be found by non-wizards and non-witches. Further, both David Eliot, the main character of *Groosham Grange*, and Harry Potter befriend a boy and girl on their first train ride to their new schools. And like David, Harry lived with a family that tormented him in a number of ways. Other commonalities exist as well, but there are many important differences, too.

For one, David actually resists the idea of being a wizard at first, while Harry does not. Additionally, the story lines of the two sets of books have little resemblance to each other, which gives them both a completely different tone and focus. Where the Groosham Grange books take a lighter look at the conflict between good and evil, the Harry Potter volumes are full of serious moments and struggles. In spite of their similarities and differences, however, both capture the imagination in their own ways and continue to have dedicated followings around the world.

named Joe Warden, who much like Horowitz, comes from a rich family and hates his grandmother, the terrible Granny.

However, Joe's grandmother is more than just a detestable person—she is actually a grotesque fiend who is actively trying to harm her grandson for the sake of her own life and that of other malicious grandmothers. Even her physical appearance and manners are revolting and can barely conceal her evil intentions. Through his detailed descriptions of Granny's disgusting habits and her wicked eccentricities, Horowitz magnifies those qualities he hated in his own grandmother and tells them with humor.

Some have compared Horowitz's work to that of Roald Dahl, author of such children's classics as *Matilda*, *Charlie and the Chocolate Factory*, and *James and the Giant Peach*.

Granny has sometimes been compared to Roald Dahl's classic *The Witches* (1983), in which a group of witches tries to carry out an evil plot against children. And indeed, it is not difficult to see how both writers enjoy including the macabre and creating characters so distorted that they can both scare and entertain. But although Horowitz enjoyed crafting these lighthearted tales, his next few books saw him slowly shifting to a different type of writing.

NEW DIRECTIONS

In his book *The Switch* (1996), Horowitz writes about two boys, one rich and one poor, who switch bodies and have the chance to experience each other's lives. Although the book still has plenty of funny moments and exaggerated characters, the two main characters, Tad Spencer and Bob Snarby, are designed to be more realistic. (Tad, the rich boy in the story, shares some similarities with Horowitz, including his favorite authors, a large home—modeled after Horowitz's own childhood residence—and wealthy parents who on the surface seem a bit like Horowitz's own.) As the story unfolds, it becomes clear that the boys are gaining new insights into themselves and the world they live in, even when facing outlandish situations or characters.

The Switch also introduces readers to the

criminal underworld of Tad's society, which in some ways resembles the portrait of England that Charles Dickens had painted in such works as *Oliver Twist*. By including observations on social class differences and making them a part of his story, Horowitz had started to change the focus of his writing. As a storyteller, Horowitz had begun to make the move away from pure children's book narratives, such as those that earned him comparisons to Roald Dahl, and toward those that incorporated themes similar to those of more adult authors, such as his favorite, Charles Dickens.

In the few years that followed *The Switch*, Horowitz began to try his hand at different types of books. In 1998, his book *The Devil and His Boy* was published. This novel is a piece of historical fiction that takes place in Elizabethan England (during the reign of Queen Elizabeth I, 1558–1603). The book includes much of the action and adventure that Horowitz loves, but because he wanted to pay attention to historical accuracy, he does not include his usual trademark humor, which makes use of wacky personalities and clever jokes (although there are plenty of enjoyable moments to be had in the book!). *The Devil and His Boy* shows a different writing style than readers of his other books may be used to—it gave Horowitz a chance to have a little fun with history, but he also does not shy away from depicting the harsh realities of life among the lower class.

Although Horowitz would continue writing his Diamond Brothers books, with their usual blend of levity and excitement, he had started a new trend of writing children's books with an edge. This had started with *The Switch*, was continued in *The Devil and His Boy*, and would be refined in many of the books that followed.

Before Horowitz turned his attention to the books that would explode his career as a children's book writer, he put out two books of horror stories, *Horowitz Horror* (1999) and *More Horowitz Horror* (2000). He had also been writing for television for several years already, which had been his primary focus. His career in writing screenplays had actually been launched after he published a book in 1985 called *The Kingfisher Book of Myths and Legends*, in which he retells famous myths and legends from around the world. Because he had learned a great deal about the legend of Robin Hood from this, he was asked to write stories for a famous British television series at the time called *Robin of Sherwood*, which established him as a screenwriter.

Soon, however, his attentions would change. As Horowitz said in an interview with authormagazine.org:

I was writing children's books that knew they were children's books. The heroes in them were having a good time. They were very easy reads…they were very fantastical. And they were doing okay, but they weren't doing great, and it occurred to me that it might be more sensible to do a slightly more serious, tougher-edged, harder book.

He continued, "Around 1999, I decided to stop doing the funny stuff and do something more serious." That was when he decided to pursue an idea he came up with ten years earlier about James Bond at age fourteen. And it was only then that Horowitz's career would really take off the way he had hoped for years.

THREE

HOROWITZ'S RISE TO FAME

D espite the fact that Horowitz did not see himself as a children's book writer for a long time, in many ways, it would seem a natural career path for him. As a young child, Horowitz did not read many big books. It was only when he grew a little older that he started picking up literary works. As a result, Horowitz recognizes that children must learn to read longer books in their own time, even if they seem challenging early on. Now, many of Horowitz's own books seem to be written to encourage such young readers—it is as though he has a natural connection with these readers because of his own childhood experiences.

A great advocate of youth reading, Horowitz sits for an interview with his children in his London home in 2006.

WRITING STYLE

By understanding the hesitation many children may have in approaching certain books, Horowitz has included elements to appeal to a broad audience in his own works. For instance, Horowitz is very aware that he is writing for a very visual generation and is always sure to include the right level of detail in his descriptions. Unlike Horowitz, children nowadays grow up with television and are used to seeing action scenes in vivid detail, complete with realistic special effects. For this reason, Horowitz tries to include as much graphic detail as possible in his works; he wants his readers to imagine each scene and adventure in their own heads so thoroughly that even a movie version of any of his books would not compare to what they see in their minds.

In addition to being able to set a scene and paint a vivid picture for his readers, Horowitz knows how to keep a story line going and has a knack for building up anticipation. He compares the story of each book to a locomotive that cannot be stopped—readers have to stay on board, so to speak, because they are curious to see what happens next.

Knowing how easy it can be to lose the interest of a young audience, Horowitz structures his books carefully so that there is never a dull moment. Even in his most thrilling works, Horowitz establishes a balance between action and dialogue, comedy and seriousness. In this way, his stories have a steady pacing so that even kids who hate reading cannot put them down.

THE RISE OF ALEX RIDER

Nowhere are these components more elegantly combined than in Horowitz's best-selling Alex Rider series. The nine books in the series follow a fourteen-year-old spy as he travels around the world on dangerous missions. The first volume, *Stormbreaker*, was published in 2000, and the series as a whole has now sold millions of copies around the world.

The idea for Alex Rider had been incubating for quite some time. The James Bond films were an important part of Horowitz's life when he was grow-ing up, and when he was younger, he would spend a great deal of time daydreaming about what it would be like to be a spy. But at a certain point, he felt that Bond should be younger. Horowitz said that when he saw actor Roger Moore in the role of Bond, he thought Bond simply looked too old, which made the films seem less appealing. This got Horowitz thinking about what it would be like to see Bond's world through the eyes of a fourteen-year-old. It was thus that Alex Rider came into being.

And sure enough, it is not difficult to see the similarities between Alex Rider and James Bond:

Ursula Andress played the character Honeychile Rider, the heroine of the James Bond film *Dr. No.*

both are agents for MI6 (Britain's intelligence agency), both are equipped with extraordinary gadgets (Alex even has pimple cream that can burn through any metal and an iPod that can hear sound through walls), both travel around the world risking their lives, and both, of course, have to face their share of villains. Horowitz has even said that the name "Rider" came about because he thought of all the women Bond had loved and figured that the one that would be the most likely to have a son with Bond would be Honeychile Rider, the heroine of *Dr. No.*

But that is where the resemblance ends. Horowitz said that even though James Bond

Sean Connery (*right*), the first actor to play James Bond in the feature films, is shown here in a scene from *Dr. No* (1962) with actor Jack Lord.

inspired the idea of Alex, he tried to make their characters vastly different. Naturally, the age difference between them is one glaring factor (at fourteen, Alex is, after all, too young to order martinis). However, there is much more to it than that. Horowitz told *Scope*, "The thing about Alex is, of course, he is not a patriot. He has no interest in serving his country…He's very much a modern teenager of this generation."

Horowitz wanted to give Alex some more dimension than his earlier characters, so while Alex in many ways is a slick hero, he is also troubled. As Horowitz wrote in the *Evening Standard*, "[Alex] suffers. The key to his appeal is surely that he doesn't actually want to be a spy.

Horowitz poses with two actors at a bookstore in London in 2005 during the launch of *Ark Angel*, the sixth volume in the Alex Rider series.

He is manipulated by adults—but, unlike me at the same age, he knows it." Horowitz has said that Alex suffers for both Horowitz and his readers; at the end of the day, Alex is still a teenage boy who wants a normal life, just as any teenager would, which allows Horowitz's young readers to identify with him.

To demonstrate Alex's vulnerability, Horowitz does not hesitate to put him in life-endangering situations that often result in Alex getting hurt or very nearly killed. Furthermore, the enemies Alex faces treat him as a legitimate threat and will not hesitate to harm him. Horowitz wants there to be a real sense of danger and threat

JAMES BOND

James Bond—also known as agent 007—the British spy created by British novelist Ian Lancaster Fleming (1908–1964), is perhaps one of the most well-known characters in popular culture. He was first introduced in Fleming's book *Casino Royale* (1953). A total of fourteen more Bond books authored by Fleming followed, as well as a string of popular movies. Bond's adeptness at fighting, outsmarting his enemies, and wooing women, all while retaining his characteristic charm and sophistication, has earned both the Bond books and movies a massive following, even to this day.

An agent for MI6, Bond is sent on missions around the world to defeat a wide variety of villains. Fleming himself worked for the British naval intelligence as a high-ranking officer during World War II, and it was his experiences there that inspired many of the events and characters in the Bond books. Interestingly, Fleming actually got the name "James Bond" from an ornithologist who wrote about the birds of Jamaica, where Fleming maintained a home (called Goldeneye) and where he spent time learning about nature.

The movie adaptations of the Bond novels have helped audiences visualize the beloved character, the adventures he has, and the incredible range of gadgets he uses. The first Bond movie, *Dr. No*, came out in 1962 and starred Sean Connery as James Bond. George Lazenby, Roger Moore, Timothy

Dalton, Pierce Brosnan, and, most recently, Daniel Craig have portrayed Bond in later movies. The films have made everything from Bond's self-introduction—"Bond. James Bond."—to the way he orders martinis—"Shaken, not stirred"—a lasting part of mainstream culture.

Several writers have taken on the challenge of following in Fleming's footsteps and writing new Bond adventures, the most recent being Jeffrey Deaver. There is also a series by Charlie Higson that follows the adventures of a young James Bond, and another by Kate Westbrook (Samantha Weinberg) that relates the life of Miss Moneypenny, the secretary of Bond's boss.

in the books so that as they go through the book, readers will have to wonder if Alex will make it or not. At the same time, Horowitz would never want to write anything dark enough to really upset or scare any of his readers. He wants his readers to feel Alex's pain in a very real sense, but at the same time, he never tries to glamorize violence or make it so extreme that it becomes distressing.

In fact, even though Alex has gadgets and has seen people die as a result of his actions, the gadgets themselves are not lethal. Moreover, despite Alex's pleas for a gun, he has never received one of his own. And in those instances where he was able to obtain one, he never actually shot and killed any-body with it.

ALEX VS. ANTHONY

While many of Horowitz's earlier characters are in part exaggerated or humorous versions of himself as a child or someone he knew, Alex is different. In fact, Horowitz chose to make Alex almost the exact opposite of himself as a child. Alex is smarter, in better shape, and more capable than Horowitz ever was. This approach seemed to pay off; as he told *NPR*, "The day I stopped drawing on the young Anthony Horowitz is the day I became successful as a writer."

However, that is not to say that Horowitz has not been inspired by episodes in his own life when writing the Alex Rider stories. "When the doorbell rings at three in the morning, it's never good news"—the very first sentence of the first Alex Rider novel, *Stormbreaker*—is actually related to the memory Horowitz has of his father's death. In the novel, the doorbell alerted Alex to the death of his uncle, Ian, an MI6 agent who had raised him. Although Ian is nothing like his father, Mark, Horowitz drew from his own emotional reactions to his father's death to help readers understand how Alex might feel.

About his own memory, Horowitz wrote in the *Observer*, "It wasn't a doorbell that rang at three o'clock, it was a telephone. I was 21 years old and living in the north London suburb of Stanmore. I knew at once what the phone call meant. It was the hospital ringing to tell us my father had died." He continues, "I gazed out of the window at the moon-light [just as Alex crosses to the window to see the police car below] and tried to think about the father I had lost."

Although Horowitz was not close to his father, he was understandably shaken by his death. It was experiencing this sense of loss that enabled him to effectively communicate Alex's reaction to his uncle's death. Horowitz wrote, "*Stormbreaker* starts with a funeral, and much of Alex's bewilderment and displacement was my own." Despite the elabo-rate action sequences and seemingly impossible situations that Alex finds himself in, it is Horowitz's ability to make him relatable that has accounted for much of Alex's—and Horowitz's—popularity.

RESEARCH

Horowitz does whatever it takes to make the books he writes enjoyable and more believable, includ-ing subjecting himself (and sometimes his family) to some strange and exotic experiences. Once, he decided to try operating a 492-foot-tall (150-meter) crane himself so that when he has Alex do it in *Point Blank*, it would be authentic. He also

Horowitz signs copies of *Snakehead*, the seventh Alex Rider volume, for adoring young fans in London in 2007.

went below the tennis courts at Wimbledon to aid in his research for *Skeleton Key*. Additionally, Horowitz makes it a point to visit every location he describes in the Alex Rider books before he actually sends Alex to them. He even makes sure that the gadgets he introduces seem plausible, despite the fact that they do not actually exist (yet). These are just some reflections of Horowitz's undying dedication and passion for his work.

THE FUTURE OF ALEX

Although his fans would surely devour a new Alex Rider adventure, Horowitz has stated that the ninth book, *Scorpia*

Rising, is the last in the series. He believes that each book he writes should be better than the one that preceded it, so he would prefer to stop writing when he feels that a body of work is as complete and perfect as it can be. He does not want to write books he is not proud of simply to make money for himself or his publishers. With *Scorpia Rising*, Horowitz felt that the series reached its logical conclusion and decided to move on to other projects.

However, fans can still check out the graphic novels that have been released of the first three Alex novels, and they can also look forward to one more tale. Horowitz has indicated that a related book about Yassen Gregorovich, the villain in several of the Alex Rider books, is in the works. He has stated that it will reveal how Yassen at fourteen made the decision to pursue a path that was the opposite of what Alex chose at the same age...and Alex himself may even make an appearance.

Horowitz told authormagazine.com, "When you become a major seller, you've only got down to go." But although he has written the last Alex Rider novel, Horowitz has retained a place in the spotlight. Even a brief look at his next undertakings and screenwriting career reveals that he has shown no signs of slowing or stopping what he does best.

OTHER ENDEAVORS AND FUTURE PROJECTS

Although Horowitz is now perhaps best known for his Alex Rider novels, his love of writing has led him to take on a wide variety of writing projects that have helped him reach new kinds of success in a wide range of genres. Horowitz has revisited his love of horror in another popular series, written a play, authored an adult novel, and maintained his long-standing career as a screenwriter. And he already has much more lined up. Nib pen in hand (Horowitz has stated that he prefers writing the way the writers he admired—Anthony Trollope and Charles Dickens—did so that he, too, can enjoy the physical experience of writing), he continues to bring the same

Horowitz sits in his spacious home office, where he often spends hours on end doing what he does best: writing.

amount of dedication to every job he has.

THE GATEKEEPERS

Just as the Alex Rider books were gaining a following among young readers, Horowitz decided to return to an idea he had long ago for another series. The Pentagram Chronicles, four books that had been published in the 1980s, were part of a fantasy series that he never finished. In them, Horowitz explored the conflict between the forces of good and the forces of evil. They are now all out of print (except in French), but armed with a fresh eye, Horowitz began revising these works for a new generation in the early 2000s. *Raven's Gate*, the first volume in the Gatekeepers series (known as the Power of Five in Britain), was published in 2005.

Horowitz's interest in writing fantasy can be traced back to his childhood. Having grown up with the Chronicles of Narnia and the Lord of the Rings, Horowitz wanted to write a fantasy series, but he also wanted to do something different. In an interview with Scholastic, he said, "I'm not very good at creating worlds. I prefer to write about the world as it is. But at the same time, it's often struck me that the real world may not be quite how we imagine it." He can walk past a church or store in his daily life, for example, and wonder what it would be like if other-worldly occurrences or sinister rituals were taking place inside without anyone else knowing. So instead of having his books take place in another world, as other fantasy writers (such as C. S. Lewis and J.R.R. Tolkien) have done in the past, Horowitz decided to place the battle for good right here on Earth.

Raven's Gate is an altered version of his earlier book, *The Devil's Doorbell* (1983), and tells the story of Matt Freeman, one of five members of a group of children known as the Gatekeepers. As Matt discovers in the book, each Gatekeeper has unique powers and is an incarnation of one of five ancient

INCA MANCO CCAPAC.

According to Incan mythology, the figure of Manco Cápac was the founder and first ruler of the city of Cuzco in Peru. He served as the inspiration for the character of Pedro in the Gatekeepers series.

Gatekeepers. Thousands of years earlier, the ancient group of five had stopped a group of evil creatures called the Old Ones from controlling humanity. However, the Old Ones reemerge and try to take over once again, and it is up to the present-day Gatekeepers to stop them as they once did.

The next books in the series, *Evil Star* (2006), *Nightrise* (2007), and *Necropolis* (2008), all introduce other members of the Gatekeepers, who hail from all over the world. Besides Matt, there is Pedro, who is from Peru; Scott and Jamie Tyler, who are twins from Nevada; and Scarlett Adams, who, like Matt, is from England, but adopted from another country. Together, they must defeat the Old Ones as they increasingly gain power in our world and attempt to spread evil. Horowitz has stated that the fifth volume in the series will be the last. The first four novels were all partly drawn from the books in the Pentagram Chronicles, but since Horowitz never finished that series, the fifth will largely contain new material.

The inspiration for the characters in the Gatekeepers series is drawn from a variety of sources. Pedro, for example, is connected to the Incan mythological figure of Manco Cápac, while Scott and Jamie are associated with figures in Native American mythology, and Scarlett is linked to a Chinese goddess. Horowitz has said that the idea for the Old Ones actually came from a nightmare he once had after his wife gave him a jug with a strange creature on the side. His dream involved his house being invaded by creatures similar to the one on the jug and triggered the idea of the Old Ones. And as for the name "Old Ones," Horowitz has said that he actually got it from a book called *Necronomicon* by H. P. Lovecraft, a writer famous for his horror, fantasy, and science fiction works.

Unlike the Alex Rider books, the Gatekeepers series involves supernatural forces, and with scenes that entail such things as blood sacrifice and other occult activities, in many ways, the series can be classified as horror as well (it has even been called Stephen King for children). In spite of their differences, however, the main characters in the Gatekeepers share a number of similarities with Alex. For one, all are orphans. Horowitz has said that he has deliberately done this to show that all of the kids must rely on themselves and their own wits to overcome the obstacles they face. In the case of the Gatekeepers, they also all have multiple identities and their ties to mythology make them timeless in a sense.

Additionally, all of the heroes are children who start off as fourteen-year-olds and turn fifteen later in the series. This is because Horowitz feels that young adults represent the future and the hope grownups have that their children will one day fix all of the problems in the world today. Moreover, even though adolescents are beginning to mature and to discover how to be adults, they still have a great deal to learn, which gives them a sense of innocence that Horowitz likes to maintain.

Despite their youth, none of Horowitz's characters are spared from violence or frightening situations. In part, this is to add suspense in each book and to indulge Horowitz's love of horror. But more than that, it also shows that his heroes experience difficulties and pain, just like everybody else.

Horowitz's desire to rewrite the Pentagram Chronicles not only represented an opportunity for him to try and perfect something he had started long ago, but also a chance to push himself as a writer. Up until he created Scarlett Adams, Horowitz had never used a female character as one of his protagonists. Given his own history with adolescent girls and the fact that he has two sons of his own, he simply felt that he could understand boys better. But the Gatekeepers, and specifically *Necropolis*, allowed Horowitz to challenge himself to explore something new. He told the *Sunday Times*, "It was inconceivable that if you have five children, one of them won't be female."

The task of writing a female character was often difficult and involved considering some important questions. For example, he had to ask if it makes Scarlett seem too weak if she were to cry. As with any character, she could not simply be a stereotypical girl with qualities that people may mistakenly assume are common in girls—those are often misleading and inappropriate. At the same time, however, readers had to be able to relate to her. In an interview with Scholastic, Horowitz said of the experience, "In the end, writing Scarlett was a pleasure. She's a little more emotional than my boy characters. She's not afraid to cry, for example. But she's also just as tough as them…I like her because she's so unpredictable."

Horowitz's adventurousness eventually proved fruitful as readers love the Gatekeepers books. They have sold considerably well and gained a following of their own. *Raven's Gate* was even made into a graphic novel. But that is not the only way Horowitz has tested his limits—always up for a new challenge, he has plunged into other types of writing, including theater and adult novels.

THEATER AND ADULT WORKS

Although Horowitz had been writing television series intended for an older audience for a long time, he had never actually attempted an adult novel before. In describing why it is sometimes difficult for a children's author to write for adults, Horowitz said that

Actors Lee Godart (*left*) and Keith Carradine starred in Horowitz's play *Mindgame* in 2008 when it ran at the Soho Playhouse in New York City.

he must consider a number of factors when writing adult characters that are not always relevant in children's stories. For example, the psychology of each character, his or her relationship to others in the book, and even where he or she lives must be very carefully thought out since these factors are more prominent in adult works. In an interview with authormagazine.org, Horowitz said, "All this sort of clutter comes into your head and I find it far harder to get that aside and get back to the actual…thrust of the story."

In contrast, he explains that children's writing tends to involve fewer details. Each detail he includes in his books for children furthers the plot and pushes the "locomotive" of the story. Instead of including elements that are secondary or not essential to the narrative, Horowitz is able to focus more on the sequence of events that are about to unfold.

Still, that did not stop him from making the leap into adult works. In 2001, Horowitz saw the publication of a play he wrote entitled *Mindgame*, a thriller that takes place in an asylum. It was performed in London's West End (the theater district of London) in 2000 and off Broadway in New York in 2008. Additionally, Horowitz's first adult novel, *The Killing Joke*, was published in 2004. It is a dark comedy that tells the story of an unemployed actor who tries to find out where jokes come from and encounters a number of unusual characters in the process. The reviews for both were mixed, and while both works received positive responses,

Horowitz is seen here in his home, where his love of literature is evident from the many volumes on the shelves.

SHERLOCK HOLMES

It is almost impossible to think about detective stories now without comparing them to the tales of detective extraordinaire Sherlock Holmes. Holmes made his debut in the 1887 tale *A Study in Scarlet*, written by Scottish writer and doctor Sir Arthur Conan Doyle (1859–1930).

Known for his keen sense of logic, the character Holmes was actually based on a professor Conan Doyle had while studying medicine at the University of Edinburgh. Dr. Joseph Bell had excellent observational and deduction skills, which he used to diagnose patients. Conan Doyle had Holmes solve crimes in much the same way in the four novels, fifty-six short stories, and one play that featured the character.

In most of the stories, Holmes's adventures are described by his close friend and assistant, Dr. John H. Watson, who recounts Holmes's ability to outsmart such villains as the criminal mastermind Professor James Moriarty. Readers quickly learn of Holmes's quirks as well as his genius and can recognize him by the cape and deerstalking cap that he is shown to wear and the pipe he is usually known to smoke. Holmes has also commonly been associated with the catchphrase, "Elementary, my dear, Watson!" but this did not actually appear in any of Conan Doyle's original works. Holmes's address, 221b Baker Street, is now the address of the official Sherlock Holmes Museum in London.

Fearing that Holmes was overshadowing his career and other works, Conan Doyle actually ended the character in 1893, only to revive him in 1902 after fans demanded to see him again. There have been numerous adaptations of Conan Doyle's works for the stage, television, and film, as well as print, but to date, only one work— Horowitz's—has been authorized by the Conan Doyle estate.

Choosing Horowitz to write the next Sherlock Holmes story was by no means random. With a number of books containing action and adventure sequences under his belt, it is obvious that Horowitz knows how to build suspense and move a plot along in a style that would fit well with the old Sherlock Holmes works. But perhaps just as telling are the television series for which Horowitz has written over the years. Given his history of writing for a number of mystery series, Horowitz would seem like a natural choice.

neither attained the type of popularity that Horowitz's children's books did.

However, despite the reactions to his earlier works and the intricacies of writing for adults, Horowitz was chosen by the Sir Arthur Conan Doyle estate to write the next Sherlock Holmes novel, 106 years after the last tale was published by Doyle. The *House of Silk*, released in November 2011, takes place in 1890 and is told from the point of view of Dr. Watson (as most of Doyle's tales were), who is actually writing it from a nursing home, a year after Holmes's death.

Horowitz sits in his office at home in 2002. In addition to writing books, he has also authored many works for the screen.

SCREENWRITING CAREER

Horowitz started his screenwriting career in the mid-1980s when he was asked to write for *Robin of Sherwood*. His love of action served him well when he wrote some episodes for the show and also helped him land jobs writing, and sometimes creating, other series. It was through many of these that Horowitz's talent for producing mystery stories became very clear.

In 1989, Horowitz began writing for *Agatha Christie's Poirot* (simply called *Poirot* in the United States), a popular television series that follows the cases of Hercule Poirot, a famous Belgian detective created by British writer Dame Agatha Christie. Horowitz adapted three of her novels and nine of

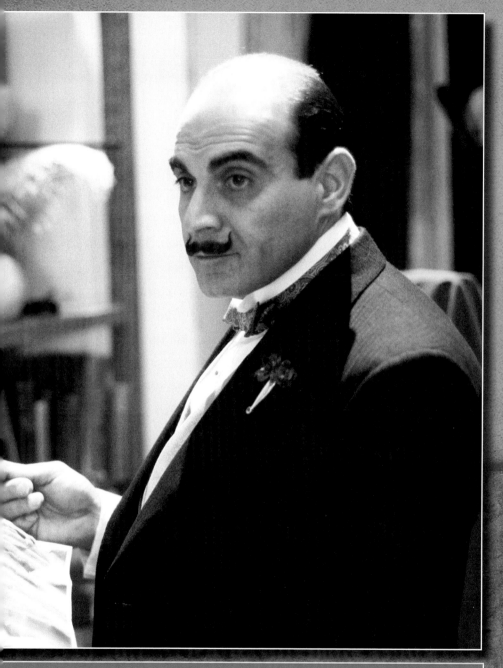

Horowitz, like many gifted authors, writes for both the page and the screen. *Agatha Christie's Poirot* was an enormously popular detective series.

her short stories for the series. Some of his greatest claims to fame, though, would come from the shows that he himself created.

In 1997, Horowitz saw the production of another mystery series called *Midsomer Murders*, which he formulated and adapted from Caroline Graham's Chief Inspector Barnaby novels. It follows the title character, Tom Barnaby (and in later episodes, Tom's cousin John), as he solves murder cases in the fictional English county of Midsomer. Horowitz went on to create one of his most acclaimed series, *Foyle's War*, about a British detective solving crimes in World War II England. He also conceived of the idea for *Collision*, a miniseries in which a number of mysteries are uncovered after a car crash. While Horowitz has worked on a number of television programs, it is perhaps these in particular that have established his reputation as a master of crime dramas.

Television screenplays are not the only screenwriting credits that Horowitz has to his name. He has tried his hand at a few films, over the years, the first major one being *The Gathering* (2002), starring Christina Ricci. He followed that up in 2006 with *Stormbreaker*, the film adaptation of his first Alex Rider novel, starring Alex Pettyfer as Alex. It was released in Britain but never made it to the United States. Although these never attained the popularity of his novels or television shows, Horowitz has not stopped. In fact, in 2011, it was announced that he would write the sequel to *The Adventures of Tintin: Secret of the Unicorn* (2011), a movie based on none other than the Tintin stories Horowitz loved so much as a child.

Although Horowitz has said that on some level, his children's books are more personal to him than his other projects, he said he enjoys screenwriting for the fact that it is fast-paced and allows him to collaborate with others (including his wife, who is a producer and has worked on a number of his shows). With screenwriting, he can leave a lot of details—such as set design—to others, and in the case of films, there is a level of excitement because of the higher budgets they have to work with. In the end, Horowitz loves all of his works equally, because, as he says, there is no point in writing if you do not write with passion.

CONTINUING SUCCESS

So how does a writer who has seen the sales of tens of millions of his books and gained a dedicated base of viewers keep himself going and ensure that his next ventures are as successful as his earlier efforts? It turns out that there is no formula—it is simply the will to keep going and to try one's hand at every opportunity that arises. Horowitz has said that the only difference between a successful writer and an unsuccessful writer is that the unsuccessful writer gave up—and as someone who endured his fair share of disappointments, Horowitz had many reasons to give up. However, he never let himself lose his passion for writing and did not use sales figures to define success. He told *NPR*, "The children's author has one duty in life, I believe, and that is always to write with hope." And throughout his career, Horowitz has done just that, inspiring not just children, but adults as well.

Since the age of eight, Horowitz has kept his pen busy, eventually turning his flair for storytelling into an almost endless stream of books, shows, and movies. With more of each on the way, Horowitz has continued to demonstrate his weight as a writer and to earn the adoration of audiences of all ages.

ON ANTHONY HOROWITZ

Name: Anthony Craig Horowitz
Birth date: April 5, 1955
Birthplace: London, England (Stanmore)
Mother: Joyce Horowitz
Father: Mark Horowitz
Spouse: Jill Green
Children: Nicholas Mark (b. 1989) and Cassian James (b. 1991)
Current residence: London, England (Clerkenwell)
Primary and secondary education: Orley Farm School, Rugby School
College: B.A., University of York, 1977
First job: Copywriter at McCann Erickson
First book published: *The Sinister Secret of Frederick K. Bower* in 1979 (also known as *Enter Frederick K. Bower*)
First screenwriting job: *Dramarama*

MAJOR AWARDS RECEIVED

Red House Children's Book Award, 2003, for *Skeleton Key*
Rebecca Caudill Young Readers' Book Award, 2004,

for *Stormbreaker*
ALA Best Book for Young Adults, 2005, for *Eagle Strike*
British Book Award (Children's Book of the Year), 2006,
  for *Ark Angel*
Bookseller Association/Nielson Author of the Year
  Award, 2007, *Ark Angel*

ON ANTHONY HOROWITZ'S WORK

BOOKS

THE DIAMOND BROTHERS MYSTERIES

The Falcon's Malteser (1986)
Public Enemy Number Two (1987)
South by South East (1997)
The French Confection (2002)
The Blurred Man (2002)
I Know What You Did Last Wednesday (2002)
Three of Diamonds (2005)
The Greek Who Stole Christmas (2007)

Series overview: The Diamond Brothers Mysteries follows the adventures of two young brothers, Tim and Nick Diamond, who run a detective agency in London. Although the brothers repeatedly find themselves in dangerous situations facing dangerous villains, plenty of humor is to be found in these volumes, which are full of references to popular culture, including classic movies and novels.

THE ALEX RIDER SERIES

Stormbreaker (2000)
Point Blank (Point Blanc) (2001)
Skeleton Key (2002)
Eagle Strike (2003)
Scorpia (2004)
Ark Angel (2005)
Snakehead (2007)
Crocodile Tears (2009)
Scorpia Rising (2011)

Series overview: The Alex Rider series features Anthony's most popular character, Alex Rider. Alex is an orphaned teenage spy for MI6 who is sent around the world on dangerous missions, where he must help defeat various criminal organizations and villains. Even as he endangers his life, Alex must deal with the everyday demands of being a teenager.

THE GATEKEEPERS (THE POWER OF FIVE)

Raven's Gate (2005)
Evil Star (2006)
Night Rise (2007)
Necropolis (2008)

Series overview: The Gatekeepers follows a group of five teenagers as they attempt to defeat evil creatures known as the Old Ones. The children are modern-day incarnations of ancient beings known as Gatekeepers, who each have special powers, and they must work together once again to save the world from evil. The fifth volume of the series is scheduled to be the conclusion.

TELEVISION

Robin of Sherwood
Poirot (Agatha Christie's Poirot)
Midsomer Murders
Foyle's War
Collision

FILMS

The Gathering (2002)
Stormbreaker (2006)

Ark Angel (2005)

"What makes the Rider books so satisfying is the way Alex gets out of situations. It's the "what would I do in such circumstances?" followed by the "I never thought of that!" that makes the series such fun, and this a welcome new addition."—*Guardian*, April, 9, 2005

Crocodile Tears (2009)

"Alex Rider's eighth adventure is one of his most ingenious, and if suitably over the top for MI6's sole teenage spy, it puts him in a world adults might recognize, with high-rolling bad guys and charities that turn out to be scams (the apt subtitle also fore-shadows a terrific scary scene alongside an infested African river)."—*New York Times*, December 17, 2009

Raven's Gate (2005)

"In this page-turner, Horowitz constantly jacks up the tension, ricocheting from catastrophe to disaster and violently killing off any adults who try to help Matt. Many of the 20 chapters end in cliffhangers, while the spectacular climax and surprising conclusion pro-vide both a satisfying ending and a good set-up for the next in the series. Go. Visit. Have an exhilarating read."—*Kirkus Reviews,* June 1, 2005

Snakehead (2007)

"Horowitz is right up there with Buchanan, Conan Doyle and H. Rider Haggard, and Alex Rider's seventh adventure proves it."—*Sunday Times*, November 9, 2007

The Switch (2004)

"While the events that transpire in this winsome adventure are delightfully absurd, the transformation that Tad undergoes strikes a genuine note. It is the young person's journey to self-definition writ large." —*Kirkus Reviews*, December 15, 2008

1955 Anthony Horowitz is born.

1963 Begins attending Orley Farm School.

1968 Begins attending Rugby School.

1973 Graduates Rugby School; begins working at Anthony Lagoon in Australia.

1974 Begins attending the University of York.

1977 Graduates from the University of York with a B.A.

1978 *Enter Frederick K. Bower (The Sinister Secret of Frederick K. Bower)* is published.

1986 Begins writing for *Robin of Sherwood*; *The Falcon's Malteser* is published.

1988 *Groosham Grange* is published; marries Jill Green.

1989 Starts writing for *Poirot (Agatha Christie's Poirot)*; Nicholas Mark Horowitz is born.

1991 Cassian James Horowitz is born.

1994 *Granny* is published.

1996 *The Switch* is published.

1997 Begins writing for *Midsomer Murders*.

1998 *The Devil and His Boy* is published.

2000 *Stormbreaker* is published; *Mindgame* opens in West End.

2002 Begins writing for *Foyle's War*.

2004 *The Killing Joke* is published.

2005 *Raven's Gate* is published.

2006 *Alex Rider: Operation Stormbreaker* (movie) is released.

2009 Begins writing for *Collision*.

2011 *Scorpia Rising* is published; *The House of Silk* is published.

ADEPTNESS Skill or proficiency in something.

ALLUSION A reference made to something that has not been directly or explicitly discussed.

CONVOLUTED Complicated or confusing.

COPYWRITER Someone who writes the text or scripts used in advertisements.

DARK COMEDY Humor involving some morbid or ironic elements.

DEPICT To show or portray something or someone in a certain, usually subjective, way.

DETESTABLE The state of being utterly unlikable or hated.

DIVERSION Something that distracts, often in an entertaining or fun way.

ECCENTRICITY A quirk or behavior that is unusual or different than the norm.

ECLECTIC Made up of assorted elements.

EMBELLISH To add false details to something to make it more appealing or attractive.

ESTATE A person's overall possessions, and in the case of an author, his or her entire body of work.

FANCY To imagine.

FORAY An attempt or venture into a new or unfamiliar area.

FORESHADOW To signal something that will happen in the future.

HEROINE The main female character in a story.

HISTORICAL ACCURACY The adherence to factual truth in history, especially pertaining to storytelling.

INCUBATE To nurture or help in the development of something.

LETHAL Deadly or able to bring about death.

LEVITY Lightheartedness or frivolity.

MALICIOUS Demonstrating malice or the intention to hurt or cause harm.

MOTLEY Made up of dissimilar or varied parts.

NARRATIVE A story or account of something.

NAYSAYER Someone who doubts, questions, or rejects something.

OBSERVATION One's perspective on something.

PATRIOT A devout supporter of one's own country.

PLAUSIBLE Seemingly believable.

PRODUCER Someone who oversees and sometimes provides the funding for a stage, television, or film production that will be viewed by the public.

PROTAGONIST Main character.

REALISTIC Representing life in a real and accurate way.

RESEMBLANCE A similar likeness to something or someone.

REVILED Spoken of with great dislike or distaste.

SADIST Someone who derives pleasure from inflicting pain or cruelty on another.

SOLICITOR A lawyer in Britain who interacts with and advises clients and can go to lower level courts on their behalf. A barrister, in contrast, is a lawyer who represents clients in higher courts but has little interaction with the client.

STEREOTYPICAL Describing a feature, habit, or behavior of a particular group, or member of that group, based primarily on overly generalized and often preju-diced views.

TRADEMARK Distinctive or characteristic of.

UNDETERRED Not discouraged or prevented from doing something.

VICTORIAN Describing attitudes, morals, or behaviors typical of or similar to those that were common in England during the reign of Queen Victoria (1837–1901). Victorian conduct was marked by strict discipline, religious morality, sexual restraint, and an overall emphasis on propriety and modesty.

VULNERABILITY Susceptibility to threat or danger.

American Library Association (ALA)
50 E. Huron
Chicago, IL 60611
(800) 545-2433
Web site: http://www.ala.org
The ALA offers information and guidance to readers
and researchers regarding any number of
acclaimed authors, such as Anthony Horowitz.

The Canadian Children's Book Centre (CCBC)
40 Orchard View Boulevard
Suite 217
Toronto, ON M4R 1B9
Canada
(416) 975-0010
Web site: http://www.bookcentre.ca
The CCBC provides resources and publications for
children's authors, teachers, and parents inter-
ested in encouraging young readers. Its programs
include TD Canadian Children's Book Week and
TD Grade One Book Giveaway.

Canadian Library Association (CLA)
1150 Morrison Drive, Suite 400
Ottawa, ON K2H 8S9
Canada
(613) 232-9625
Web site: http://www.cla.ca
The Canadian Library Association advocates for the
nation's library network and provides support to
Canadian authors.

Centauri Summer Arts Camp
Centauri at the RLA
RR3
Wellandport, ON L0R 2J0
Canada
(416) 766-7124
Web site: http://www.centauriartscamp.com
Centauri offers a variety of programs, including several
    writing workshops, to encourage a love of all arts
    among young people.

Children's Book Council (CBC)
54 West 39th Street, 14th Floor
New York, NY 10018
(212) 966-1990
Web site: http://www.cbcbooks.org
The Children's Book Council is a nonprofit organization
    whose goal is to expose book lovers to the
    variety of new and established children's and
    young adult authors.

826 National
44 Gough Street
Suite 206
San Francisco, CA 94103
(415) 864-2098
Web site: http://www.826national.org
826 National offers tutoring programs and workshops
    around the United States for students who are
    seeking to improve their writing skills and to refine
    their creative voice.

Library of Congress
101 Independence Ave SE
Washington, DC 20540
Web site: http://www.loc.gov
The Library of Congress keeps records of all books
    published in the United States and offers research
    assistance to the public upon request.

Penguin Books
375 Hudson Street
New York, NY 10014
(212) 366-2000
Web site: http://us.penguingroup.com
Penguin Books has published many of Horowitz's
    books in the United States and provides informa-
    tion on the author and his works.

Publishers Weekly
71 West 23rd Street, #1608
New York, NY 10010
(212) 377-5500
Web site: http://www.publishersweekly.com
As one of the top industry magazines of the book
    publishing industry, *Publishers Weekly* offers
    insights on emerging trends, author interviews,
    and reviews of upcoming titles.

Random House Children's Books
1745 Broadway
New York, NY 10019
(212) 782-9000

Web site: http://www.randomhouse.com/kids/
home.pperl
Random House is the largest publisher of trade books
in the world and has an extensive roster of
authors of young adult titles, including many of
Anthony Horowitz's peers.

Scholastic, Inc.
557 Broadway
New York, NY 10012
(212) 343-6100
Web site: http://www.scholastic.com
Scholastic has published the Gatekeepers books in
the United States and offers information about
the author and his works as well as engaging
online activities and quizzes related to many of
the books.

Society of Children's Book Writers & Illustrators (SCBWI)
8271 Beverly Boulevard
Los Angeles, CA 90048
(323) 782-1010
Web site: http://www.scbwi.org
The Society of Children's Book Writers & Illustrators is
a revered organization whose members include
some of the premier children's writers and artists.

Thurber House
77 Jefferson Avenue
Columbus, OH 43215
(614) 464-1032

Web site: http://www.thurberhouse.org
Thurber House offers a number of programs year-round for writers of all ages seeking to hone their writing skills.

Vancouver Public Library (VPL)
350 West Georgia Street
Vancouver, BC V6B 6B1
Canada
(604) 331-3603
Web site: http://www.vpl.ca
The VPL provides a number of resources for aspiring writers, including a Writing and Book Camp for young adults.

Walker Books
87 Vauxhall Walk
London, England SE11 5HJ
+44 (0) 20 7793 0909
Web site: http://www.walker.co.uk
Walker Books has published many of Horowitz's books in Britain and provides information on the author, his works, awards he has won, and his public appearances.

Young Adult Library Services Association (YALSA)
50 E. Huron Street
Chicago, IL 60611
(800) 545-2433, ext. 4390
Web site: http://www.ala.org/ala/mgrps/divs/yalsa/yalsa.cfm

YALSA, part of the American Library Association, aims to expose young people to the world of books and emerging authors through its programs such as Teen Read Week.

WEB SITES

Due to the changing nature of Internet links, Rosen Publishing has developed an online list of Web sites related to the subject of this book. This site is updated regularly. Please use this link to access the list:

http://www.rosenlinks.com/AAA/Horo

Alexie, Sherman, and Ellen Forney. *The Absolutely True Diary of a Part-time Indian*. New York, NY: Little, Brown, 2009.

Alexie, Sherman. *War Dances*. New York, NY: Grove, 2009.

Blyton, Enid. *The Island of Adventure*. 1944. Reprint. London, England: Macmillan, 2006.

Colfer, Eoin. *Artemis Fowl*. New York, NY: Hyperion Books, 2001.

Collins, Suzanne. *Catching Fire, Book Two*. New York, NY: Scholastic, 2009.

Collins, Suzanne. *The Hunger Games*. New York, NY: Scholastic, 2008.

Collins, Suzanne. *Mockingjay*. New York, NY: Scholastic, 2010.

Dahl, Roald. *Charlie and the Chocolate Factory*. 1964. Reprint. New York, NY: Penguin Books, 2011.

Dahl, Roald. *The Witches*. 1983. Reprint. New York, NY: Penguin Books, 2007.

Deaver, Jeffery. *Carte Blanche*. New York, NY: Simon & Schuster, 2011.

Dickens, Charles. *David Copperfield*. 1850. Reprint. London, England: Penguin Books, 2004.

Dickens, Charles. *Oliver Twist*. 1837. Reprint. London, England: Penguin Books, 2009.

Doyle, Arthur Conan. *A Study in Scarlet*. New York, NY: Penguin Books, 2007.

Fleming, Ian. *Casino Royale*. New York, NY: Penguin Books, 2002.

Hergé. *Tintin in the Land of the Soviets*. San Francisco,

CA: Last Gasp of San Francisco, 2003.

Higson, Charlie. *SilverFin*. New York, NY: Hyperion Books, 2005.

Horowitz, Anthony. *The Devil and His Boy*. New York, NY: Penguin Books, 1998.

Horowitz, Anthony. *The Falcon's Malteser*. 1986. Reprint. New York, NY: Penguin Books, 2004.

Horowitz, Anthony. *Granny*. New York, NY: Penguin Books, 1994.

Horowitz, Anthony. *Groosham Grange*. 1988. Reprint. New York, NY: Penguin Books, 2008.

Horowitz, Anthony. *The House of Silk*. New York, NY: Hachette, 2011.

Horowitz, Anthony. *Raven's Gate*. New York, NY: Scholastic, 2005.

Horowitz, Anthony. *Stormbreaker*. New York, NY: Penguin Books, 2000.

King, Stephen. *The Gunslinger*. New York, NY: Penguin Books, 2003.

Lewis, C. S. *The Lion, the Witch, and the Wardrobe*. New York, NY: HarperCollins, 2000.

Meyer, Stephenie. *Breaking Dawn*. New York, NY: Little, Brown, 2011.

Meyer, Stephenie. *Eclipse*. New York, NY: Little, Brown, 2010.

Meyer, Stephenie. *The Host: A Novel*. New York, NY: Little, Brown, 2011.

Meyer, Stephenie. *New Moon*. New York, NY: Little, Brown, 2009.

Meyer, Stephenie. *Twilight*. New York, NY: Little, Brown, 2008.

Paver, Michelle. *Wolf Brother*. New York, NY: HarperCollins, 2004.

Price, Willard. *Adventure Double: Diving and Amazon Adventures*. London, England: Red Fox, 1993.

Riordan, Rick. *The Lost Hero*. New York, NY: Disney/Hyperion, 2010.

Riordan, Rick. *The Serpent's Shadow*. New York, NY: Disney/Hyperion, 2012.

Riordan, Rick. *The Son of Neptune*. New York, NY: Disney/Hyperion, 2011.

Sachar, Louis. *Holes*. 1998. Reprint. New York, NY: Macmillan, 2008.

Tolkien, J.R.R. *The Fellowship of the Ring: Being the First Part of the Lord of the Rings*. New York, NY: Random House, 2005.

Westbrook, Kate. *The Moneypenny Diaries*. New York, NY: Macmillan, 2005.

Abrams, Dennis. *Anthony Horowitz*. New York, NY: Infobase Publishing, 2006.

AnthonyHorowitz.com. "Interview with BBC Radio 5." April 6, 2011. Retrieved October 3, 2011 (http://anthonyhorowitz.com/newscentre/alexrider/anthony-horowitz-on-bbc-radio-5-live-06-april-2011/271/).

Ardagh, Philip. "Alex Rides Again." *Guardian*, April 9, 2005. Retrieved October 3, 2011 (http://www.guardian.co.uk/books/2005/apr/09/featuresreviews.guardianreview30).

Authormagazine.org. "Horowitz Interview." Online video interview. Retrieved October 3, 2011 (http://www.authormagazine.org/interviews/Horowitz_Interview_Part_1.mov) (http://www.authormagazine.org/interviews/Horowitz_Interview_Part_2.mov) (http://www.authormagazine.org/interviews/Horowitz_Interview_Part_3.mov).

BBC. "The Interview: 07/08/09 Anthony Horowitz." BBC World Service, August 7, 2009. Retrieved October 3, 2011 (http://www.bbc.co.uk/iplayer/console/p003v192).

Campbell, Liza. "Anthony Horowitz: My Family Values." *Guardian*, July 10, 2010. Retrieved October 3, 2011 (http://www.guardian.co.uk/lifeandstyle/2010/jul/10/anthony-horowitz-alex-rider).

CITV.com. "Anthony Horowitz!" Retrieved October 3, 2011 (http://www.citv.co.uk/page.asp?partid=280).

Craig, Amanda. "Snakehead by Anthony Horowitz." *Sunday Times*, November 9, 2007. Retrieved

October 3, 2011 (http://entertainment.timesonline
.co.uk/tol/arts_and_entertainment/books/children/
article2839512.ece).

Crompton, Sarah. "I Knew that Alex Was Special from
the First." *Telegraph*, March 30, 2005. Retrieved
October 3, 2011 (http://www.telegraph.co.uk/
culture/books/3639520/I-knew-that-Alex-was-
special-from-the-first.html).

Forshaw, Barry. "Anthony Horowitz: Growing Up in
Public." *Independent*, August 13, 2004.
Retrieved October 3, 2011 (http://www
.independent.co.uk/arts-entertainment/books/
features/anthony-horowitz-growing-up-in
-public-556381.html).

Guardian. "Anthony Horowitz: 'I Had No Plan B. I Was
Going to Be a Writer or Nothing'—Video." April
21, 2011. Retrieved October 3, 2011 (http://www
.guardian.co.uk/childrens-books-site/video/2011/
apr/21/anthony-horowitz-video).

Horowitz, Anthony. "Anthony Horowitz: Why Am I Killing
Off My Hero? It's Elementary, of Course!" *Daily
Mail*, March 25, 2011. Retrieved October 3, 2011
(http://www.dailymail.co.uk/femail/article-1369628/
Anthony-Horowitz-Why-I-killing-hero-It-s-
elementary-course.html).

Horowitz, Anthony. "My Perfect Weekend: Anthony
Horowitz." *Telegraph*, March 24, 2011. Retrieved
October 3, 2011 (http://www.telegraph.co.uk/news/
celebritynews/my-perfect-weekend/8404311/
My-perfect-weekend-Anthony-Horowitz.html).

Horowitz, Anthony. "Once Upon a Life: Anthony Horowitz." *Observer*, April 3, 2011. Retrieved October 3, 2011 (http://www.guardian.co.uk/lifeandstyle/2011/apr/03/once-upon-a-life-anthony-horowitz).

Horowitz, Anthony. "Perils of Privilege." *London Evening Standard*, March 24, 2003. Retrieved October 3, 2011 (http://www.thisislondon.co.uk/showbiz/article-3979259-perils-of-privilege.do).

Ian Fleming Official Site. Retrieved October 3, 2011 (http://www.ianfleming.com/pages/content/index.asp?PageID=268).

Jacques, Adam. "Anthony Horowitz: I'm Phobic About Dying in the Middle of Writing a Book." *Independent*, April 3, 2011. Retrieved October 3, 2011 (http://www.independent.co.uk/arts-entertainment/books/features/anthony-horowitz-im-phobic-about-dying-in-the-middle-of-writing-a-book-2257508.html).

Just, Julie. "Alex Rider: Crocodile Tears." *New York Times*, December 17, 2009. Retrieved October 3, 2011 (http://www.nytimes.com/2009/12/20/books/review/Bookshelf-t.html?ref=bookreviews).

Kellaway, Kate. "Boy's Own Hero." *Observer*, April 10, 2005. Retrieved October 3, 2011 (http://www.guardian.co.uk/books/2005/apr/10/booksforchildrenandteenagers.comment).

Kennedy, Maev. "New Sherlock Holmes Novel by Anthony Horowitz Out in November." *Guardian*, April 12, 2011. Retrieved October 3, 2011

(http://www.guardian.co.uk/books/2011/apr/12/
sherlock-holmes-novel-anthony-horowitz).

Kirkus Reviews. "Raven's Gate." June 1, 2005.
Retrieved October 3, 2011 (http://www
.kirkusreviews.com/book-reviews/childrens-
books/anthony-horowitz/ravens-gate/#review).

Kirkus Reviews. "The Switch." December 15, 2008.
Retrieved October 3, 2011 (http://www
.kirkusreviews.com/book-reviews/childrens-
books/anthony-horowitz/the-switch/#review).

Naish, John. "Anthony Horowitz: Why I'm Writing About
Girls." *Sunday Times*, November 1, 2008.
Retrieved October 3, 2011 (http://www
.timesonline.co.uk/tol/life_and_style/health/
article5054924.ece).

NPR.org "Thrilled to Death." August 4, 2010.
Retrieved October 3, 2011 (http://www.npr.org/
templates/story/story.php?storyId=128515960).

Purdon, Fiona. "Anthony Horowitz Has Lost His Role
Models for Alex Rider." *Courier Mail*, November
18, 2008. Retrieved October 3, 2011 (http://www
.couriermail.com.au/entertainment/books/
horowitzs-amazing-ride/
story-e6freqkx-1111118016681).

Rabinovitch, Dina. "Author of the Month: Anthony
Horowitz." *Guardian*, June 25, 2003. Retrieved
October 3, 2011 (http://www.guardian.co.uk/
books/2003/jun/25/
booksforchildrenandteenagers.dinarabinovitch).

Scholastic Book Club. "Interview with Anthony
Horowitz!" Retrieved October 3, 2011

(http://clubs-kids.scholastic.co.uk/
    clubs_content/2748).
Scope. "An Interview with Anthony Horowitz." August
    15, 2006. Retrieved October 3, 2011
    (http://www2.scholastic.com/browse/article
    .jsp?id=7245).
Teenreads.com. "Anthony Horowitz: Author Talk." April
    2009. Retrieved October 3, 2011 (http://www
    .teenreads.com/authors/au-horowitz-anthony
    .asp).

ABOUT THE AUTHOR

Shalini Saxena received her undergraduate degree from Cornell University and a master's degree from Georgetown University. Always an avid reader, she now works as an editor and writer. She currently lives in New York City.

PHOTO CREDITS